WHAT'S NEXT? **?** WHAT'S NEXT?

THE FUTURE OF
Warfare

By Diane Bailey

W
FRANKLIN WATTS
LONDON • SYDNEY

Contents

INTRODUCTION

The soldiers on the battlefield are assessing the situation, looking for enemy troops, bombs or other weapons. Even when the temperature soars, these soldiers do not sweat. And when the battle lasts for days without pause, their senses remain as sharp as ever. They never doubt what they have to do. And even if they 'die', there will be no one to mourn them, because these soldiers are not human. They are battery-powered machines operated by computer chips. Armed and dangerous, able to process billions of pieces of information in a second, these new soldiers fight for humans, but on the front lines, it's only machines that are at risk. This is a war of robots – and it may start to become a reality in as little as a decade.

Robots haven't yet completely replaced human soldiers, but remotely operated robots and vehicles (ROVs) are already turning up in war zones across the world. Meanwhile, researchers in the United States, Korea, Japan and the European Union are working to develop even more robots – models that look like anything from humans to hummingbirds! Robots are just one part of future warfare. New military technology will lead to the development of more accurate and powerful weapons. Further research and development will also focus on better communications, as soldiers will be able use the Internet to receive information, even in the heat of battle. In the future, the biggest battles may not be about land or politics, but about improving the technology to fight for them.

The armed forces in the United States lead the world in the use of robots and ROVs, deploying some that can manipulate other objects (above) and some designed to detect chemicals (left).

CHAPTER ONE · CHAPTER ONE

A WORLD AT WAR

People have been fighting each other since the first humans evolved. Some fights are over food or territory. Others are about religion or political ideas. Over time, humans have become much more skilled at waging war, improving their physical strength, intelligence, skills at trickery – and especially technology.

Technological inventions have fuelled the progress of war for centuries. As people developed weapons, tools and other equipment, warfare changed. For example, the invention of the saddle – and later the stirrup – improved the ability of warriors on horseback to wield their weapons more effectively. Being able to wage war on horseback also offered a soldier more speed, power and protection than fighting on foot with swords or blunt instruments such as clubs.

Missile weapons were another step forward. From slingshots to bows and arrows, weapons that travelled through the air let people fight from a distance and launch surprise attacks. One of the ultimate projectile weapons is the bullet. Gunpowder was invented in China in the 10th century AD. It took a few hundred years, but this explosive substance eventually ended up not only in huge cannons but also in hand-held firearms. First used in the 13th century, guns changed the image of the soldier. Their success in battle was no longer directly linked to physical condition. A tired soldier could still fire a gun, even if he (or she) wasn't able to wield a sword.

Improvements in construction methods and transportation also changed how wars were fought. In the distant past, boats were rowed by people. But then the invention of the sail put the wind to

The invention of gunpowder, used in cannons (left) and smaller firearms, greatly reduced the need for hand-to-hand combat and changed warfare for ever.

work instead. Wooden boats were vulnerable when they faced an enemy ship with a powerful cannon that could blast holes in a hull or start a fire. But stronger steel boats could better defend themselves. By the middle of the 19th century, trains were also revolutionising warfare. They could travel faster and carry more food and equipment than an army travelling on foot. During the American Civil War (1861–65), both the Union and Confederate armies relied on the railways to move soldiers and supplies.

Trains were fast, but early tanks were not. These ground vehicles, which featured both big guns and heavy armour, moved slowly, but they were powerful and durable weapons. In 1904, British inventor David Roberts developed the idea of a vehicle that used circular 'crawler tracks'. Later, a British army officer, Ernest Swinton, convinced his government to try using tanks in World War I (1914–18). During this war, thousands of tanks were used to help the soldiers advance from the trenches and to attack the enemy, but the tanks were still outnumbered by the number of horses used. However, it was not until World War II (1939–45) and the advancements in tank technology that their real power was revealed. Germany used tanks as part of its *blitzkrieg* ('lightning war') strategy. The Germans combined tanks, foot soldiers and air support to blast through enemy lines. "The real story here is not just about the technology, but about how various armies have adapted or not adapted to this new technology, and about these

commanders struggling with innovations," said American military historian Max Boot.

As troops became better protected and more mobile, it became even more important for an army to know what its enemy was doing. Spies who infiltrate enemy ranks, intercept orders and gather information have always been vital to success in warfare. In 1794, the French army launched the first reconnaissance aircraft – a hot-air balloon. Using technology developed by French scientist Jean-Marie-Joseph Coutelle, the French spied on their enemies, the Austrians, from above, writing down information and dropping it to soldiers on the ground. This aerial observation helped bring about a military victory for France in the Battle of Fleurus.

Communications devices, such as the telegraph, also helped to develop the way wars were fought, since they enabled information to be relayed more quickly and reliably without the aid of a messenger on horseback. Later, the telephone, two-way radios and computers would increasingly make communicating faster and easier. Sending messages using secret codes was one way to evade enemy infiltration, but this was not foolproof. During both world wars, specialist code breakers (cryptographers) were in great demand.

The 20th century witnessed a surge of global warfare – and with it a surge in the technology used to wage those battles. Aeroplanes were first used for reconnaissance during World War I, and some

A new age of warfare dawned in August 1945, when the *Enola Gay* (right) dropped an atomic bomb on Hiroshima, Japan. Three days later, the Japanese city of Nagasaki was also bombed (above).

aircraft were tested as remote-controlled weapons. The US Army asked an inventor, Charles Kettering, to design an unmanned flying machine that could carry a bomb and hit a target 64 kilometres away. The result was the Kettering Bug, a lightweight biplane. However, the war ended before the 'Bug' was ever engaged in combat.

Aerial technology made a big leap forward 25 years later, during World War II. Engineers in Germany, the UK and other nations developed powerful new weapons and technologies, including the first jet-powered fighter plane. Germany unveiled the V-1, an unmanned 'flying bomb' that could travel faster than a traditional plane and carry more weight. Later they also introduced the V-2 rocket, a long-range ballistic missile. The V-1 had more impact on the war, but the V-2 set the stage for developing future ballistic missiles – including those that could carry an atomic warhead.

World War II saw the first use of the atomic bomb, which was developed by the US government's Manhattan Project, led by scientist J Robert Oppenheimer. Fuelled by nuclear power, the atomic bomb was the most powerful weapon the world had ever seen, unmatched in its destructive capability. Not only could a single bomb's explosion kill hundreds of thousands of people, but its after-effects were also deadly. Nuclear explosions release radiation that spreads through the air. It causes radiation sickness, which can lead to death. During the 1950s and 1960s, with World War II in the recent past, the world's superpowers – particularly the United States and the Soviet Union – raced to develop more nuclear weapons. During this fearful five-decade period, known as the 'Cold War', citizens around the world lived with the fear that their lives might be ended simply by the push of a button, releasing hundreds of nuclear warheads.

Nuclear weapons are categorised as weapons of mass destruction (WMD). But biological and chemical weapons also fall within this

category. During World War I, the use of a poison called mustard gas brought extreme pain and sometimes death to many soldiers. Chlorine gas was also used. Throughout history, biological warfare has also been waged by spreading the germs of fatal diseases such as anthrax. Today, the use of such weapons is mostly outlawed by international treaties.

In 1991, the United States and a group of allied countries went to war with Iraq during the first Gulf War – a conflict that has been called the first 'information age' war. The United States' armed forces used computers to help direct soldiers' movements as well

AIMING TO SAVE LIVES

Killing is one of the major strategies of war, but it's usually done to make a point, to change a nation's political system and to gain control. Some new inventions will make it easier to kill, but others will let soldiers repel or evade an enemy without lethal force. Historically, many ordinary civillians have died as a result of conflict. But better technologies should allow the armed forces to focus their weaponry with greater accuracy on military targets. This will reduce the risk to any civilians who live within a war zone. Military personnel also hope that new advances – such as unmanned machines – will reduce the number of casualties that 'friendly forces' suffer, since they won't have to enter hostile territory.

Combat aircraft take many forms; America's A-10 Thunderbolt (opposite) was designed for close air support, or attacking targets on the ground from close range.

TESLA'S WAR BOATS

In 1898, Serbian-American inventor Nikola Tesla demonstrated a 1.8 metre-long remote-controlled boat that he called a 'teleautomaton'. He operated it while standing several metres away. Tesla believed that a fleet of several hundred such boats could be armed with weapons and could then attack warships. Tesla wrote in his autobiography, "I really thought that it would abolish war, because of its unlimited destructiveness and exclusion of the personal element of combat." Neither the US Navy nor the British Royal Navy– then among the world's strongest forces – were interested at the time, but Tesla's ideas eventually contributed to the development of other remote-controlled weapons.

as to analyse surveillance photos taken by satellites. In 1995, information warfare took another leap forward when computers were integrated with the Global Positioning System (GPS), which allows soldiers to pinpoint their exact locations on a map and navigate through unfamiliar territory.

The second half of the 20th century saw new developments in not only weapons and technology but also in the types of wars being fought. Up to and including World War II, conventional warfare reigned. Wars were between countries. They were fought by uniformed military personnel in specific war zones – on land, at sea and in the air. During the 1950s, the rules of warfare changed, and many conflicts became unconventional. A soldier's opponent might not be another soldier from a different country. Instead, it might be a terrorist group, a political leader or even a civilian. In Afghanistan, some soldiers have fought this type of war, where the goal is to curtail terrorist activity by organisations such as al-Qaeda. In this new type of war, the dangers are both known and unknown, and the soldiers who fight it require better tools than ever before.

Modern warfare often involves surveillance by satellites (carried into space by rockets, pictured left) and stealth aircraft such as the recently retired B-2 Spirit (below).

INTELLIGENT WARFARE

Today's armed forces don't always know what they're up against. Threats may come from anyone and from anywhere. War cannot always be avoided, but increasingly, it can be fought from a distance. Unmanned aerial vehicles (UAVs) were first developed during World War I, and they continued to be deployed throughout the 20th century. Although they were originally developed to conduct surveillance, in the early 2000s some were modified to fire weapons. An American UAV called the Predator was equipped with Hellfire missiles, and many of these small planes have been used to attack and kill al-Qaeda members in Afghanistan and Iraq. These planes carry no people on board, as they are remotely guided by pilots who can be located a long way – or even a continent – away.

The US armed forces have increasingly used the Predator (pictured opposite and above) in the war against terrorists. The remote-controlled UAV is hard for enemies to spot and reduces the risk to US personnel.

ARMED, DANGEROUS AND AUTONOMOUS

As UGVs, UAVs and robots are becoming more able to act on their own, a debate is growing over whether they should be allowed to carry guns or other weapons. Currently, technology is not advanced enough to ensure that a robot could be programmed to make the same decisions that a human could. If the robot makes a deadly mistake, who should be held responsible? Should it be the robot's software designer or the commanding officer who sent it into combat? As military expert P W Singer points out, "Technology

Unmanned ground vehicles are a modern army's workhorses, designed to remotely launch missiles (opposite) or to lighten soldiers' loads by carrying equipment (left).

Armed forces around the world are relying more and more on unmanned aerial vehicles, or UAVs (sometimes called drones) and other types of robots. In 2013, P W Singer, a military expert, calculated that alongside the United States there were 76 countries with military robotics programmes. However, the United States leads the world in the use of such technology. A decade ago, it had about 50 UAVs; today it has about 7,000. In addition, it has another 12,000 unmanned ground vehicles (UGVs).

During World War I, soldiers attacked the enemy from trenches dug in on each side of the battlefield. Today, an increasing number of military personnel may be found in air-conditioned office buildings filled with computers. The enemy is in front of these soldiers in the form of images being broadcast through their computer monitors. With a headset, a keyboard and a joystick, these pilots can operate remote-controlled vehicles that are stationed thousands of kilometres away from the war zone. Although these 'cubicle warriors' can kill from their seats, they cannot be killed. For them, the drive to and from work every day is more dangerous than the battle itself. According to P W Singer, "Every previous revolution in war… was about a system that either shot faster, went further, [or] had a bigger boom. That's certainly the case with robotics, but they also change the experience of the warrior and even the very identity of the warrior."

Robots are good at doing what people can't do or don't want to do. They don't care if a task is boring or dangerous, and they're not nearly as demanding as people. They don't need to eat, sleep or relax. As one promotional advertisement for an unmanned plane asked, "Can you keep your eyes open for thirty hours without blinking?"

In wars in countries such as Afghanistan, improvised explosive devices (IEDs) – often planted along roadsides – have caused most of the deaths among the allied forces. But a new force of warriors – more than 5,000 strong – is helping to combat IEDs. PackBots are military UGV that can survey dangerous areas and locate and disable bombs. The 'Warrior' is five times bigger than a PackBot, but it can still fit through a door and climb a flight of stairs. It's also extremely versatile, it has a USB port that lets it use a gun, specialised sensors… or even an iPod and speakers! Both the PackBot and the Warrior resemble small tanks carrying a mechanical arm. The TALON is an UGV that can drive through snow and sand and even go underwater. It is fast enough to keep up with a person running. It is mainly used to assist with bomb disposal operations. A version of TALON with a Special

Military robots can be especially valuable in detecting enemy traps – specifically, IEDs (simulated in training, opposite) and hazardous materials such as chemicals (below).

Weapons Observation Reconnaissance Detection System (SWORDS) came with a gun-mount and could be remotely operated by a soldier. SWORDS UGVs are no longer being made, but a more advanced model is in development.

In 2006, researchers at the National Robotics Engineering Center at Pennsylvania's Carnegie Mellon University, USA, unveiled the Crusher. The Crusher is an unmanned tank, weighing 5.9 tonnes and can carry 3.6 tonnes of cargo or weapons. It can reach speeds of 42 kilometres per hour and roll over a 1.2 metre-high wall. Prototypes of other robotic machines look like characters straight out of the *Transformers* films. The Big Dog, for example, is designed to walk; it can climb hills, navigate muddy trails, wade through water and keep its balance on rocks. Because it can go where normal vehicles cannot, it's ideal for difficult terrain.

Yet for all of its benefits, combat robotics does have its downside. In 2007, an armed robot in South Africa malfunctioned during a demonstration. The robot cannon, which was programmed to act without direct human input, turned its gunfire onto friendly soldiers, killing nine of them. Despite such setbacks, robotic vehicles are gaining popularity in armed forces around the world because, in general, they let human soldiers stay in safer places. The F-35, a manned fighter jet, was launched in 2006 and became the US Air Force's most advanced plane. However, Robert Gates, the US Secretary of Defence from 2006 to 2011, has said that the F-35 will probably be the last manned fighter aircraft developed for the US Air Force.

Former Secretary of Defense Robert Gates (left) and other US military officials believe that the F-35 fighter jet (above) represents the end of an era in aircraft built for war.

Part explosive and part computer, today's 'smart bombs' are an entirely different class of weapon from the fuse-triggered bombs used in war a century ago.

BUILDING METAL BRAINS

American engineer James Albus built machines and computer networks that can mimic the brain, and his theories and models for 'intelligent systems' have been the foundation for several military robots and unmanned vehicles. The Real-Time Control System, which he helped invent, outlines what man-made 'minds' have to do and in what order. The system has been used in a variety of projects – some involving unmanned, underwater vehicles, others involving postal systems in the US Postal Service. Albus, who died in 2011, worked as a senior robotics scientist at Robotic Technology Incorporated in Washington DC, and pointed out that robots can be less trouble than humans. "Train one or two and you can download a CD to the others," he said.

Shortly after it was invented, the gun – in all its shapes and sizes – has been the primary weapon in war. However, there's a new kid on the block: precision-guided munitions (PGMs), or 'smart bombs'. These bombs can be controlled remotely and guided through the air to their targets. Unlike previous missiles, these can be steered, and adjustments made if necessary, even after they have left the ground. PGMs are designed to reduce 'collateral damage', by their ability to pinpoint a target with greater accuracy and reduce likelihood of casualties to civillians and allied forces on the ground.

Armed forces now rely heavily on accurate information about their circumstances, and they need to have a way of communicating with each other. Currently, American and British forces use a system called 'Blue Force Tracking'. 'Blue forces' are friendly soldiers. Blue Force Tracking is a GPS program that communicates with satellites. Using it, soldiers can determine their location and find other troops.

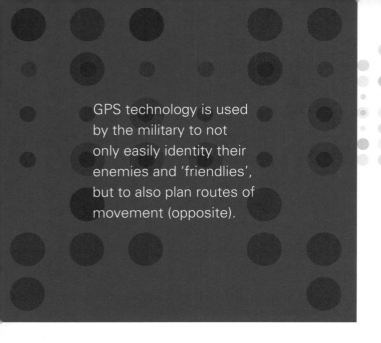

GPS technology is used by the military to not only easily identity their enemies and 'friendlies', but to also plan routes of movement (opposite).

They can also send messages to each other. However, these systems still have weaknesses. Smoke, bad weather and rough terrain can all interfere with such high-tech systems. Also, the tools of one army often become the tools of another. GPS was initially developed by the United States Department of Defense, but GPS is now widely available to anyone, including enemy forces.

Cyberspace has been called the new war zone. Computers and the Internet allow huge amounts of all kinds of information to be spread almost instantaneously across the world. Today's wars are 'network-centric', meaning they rely on sharing information through technology. While information is an invaluable tool in warfare, it also has the potential to be a drawback. Today's military are sometimes presented with huge amounts of information. This can lead to 'information overload', making it difficult to know what is a priority and what needs to be taken care of immediately. Sometimes critical information can get overlooked. In addition, it can be difficult to keep information secure from hackers breaking into computer networks.

WAR 2.0

Robots, smart weapons and information technology are changing how wars are fought, but there are still humans on the battlefield – and protecting them remains the top priority. By as early as 2020, soldiers could have bodysuits capable of everything from repelling bullets to seeking out enemy soldiers. For example, these suits might have thermal sensors that can detect if people are nearby and then send the information to a video screen encased in the soldier's helmet. The suit might surround a layer of liquid armour that will harden if a bullet makes contact, protecting the soldier from injury. The suit's outer layer might automatically change colour to provide camouflage, while the inner layer might heat up or cool down, depending on the weather. Sensors might measure the soldier's temperature and heart rate and tell him if anything is wrong. These special suits may even increase a soldier's natural physical abilities, allowing him to lift heavier loads or jump further.

The soldier of the future may also carry new types of weapons. Directed energy (DE) weapons use lasers and microwaves. Many weapons popular in science-fiction are laser-powered. Travelling at the speed of light, lasers are far faster than even the fastest bullet. Laser weapons are also cleaner and cheaper. Although not yet in widespread use, such weapons are constantly being tested and refined and could be a standard weapon within 5 to 10 years. Doug Beason, an American physicist and retired US Air Force officer, writes, "When [DE weapons] are unleashed on the battlefield, they'll be more revolutionary than the longbow, machine gun, stealth

Today, lasers are used mainly in targeting rather than as a weapon in themselves; they may be used as range-finders on rifles (above) or in missile guidance systems (left).

So far, the Active Denial System (informally called the 'heat ray') has seen little use in military combat, but it has proved itself to be useful in controlling urban riots and even prison fights.

aeroplane, cruise missile, nuclear submarine or atomic bomb. The Second Gulf War may well be the last *not* to depend on directed energy."

One DE weapon is the Active Denial System developed by the US armed forces. This system creates radio waves that generate a painful feeling of extreme heat, forcing people to instinctively back away. Unlike conventional weapons, it does not kill, making it an option for either repelling enemy forces or controlling rowdy crowds. Other non-lethal weapons involve sounds and smells. For example, filling an area with a disgusting smell, such as sewage or decaying flesh, can drive away enemies. Loud or obnoxious sounds can also break up crowds. And sounds that are beyond the audible range can have adverse effects, causing nausea and confusion. Non-lethal weapons are already in use, but they may play an even bigger role in future warfare because they will be legal to use, according to international treaty, whereas more powerful chemical or biological weapons are not. Also, non-lethal weapons are preferable in combat locations that are close to civilian populations.

Another type of weapon is in development by the US armed forces and could be ready by about 2025. The concept is rather simple as it is a kind of advanced form of the slingshot. A tungsten or titanium rod, measuring about 6 metres-long and 3 metres in diameter would be launched from a satellite in space. The satellite could be programmed fire the rod at a specific target on Earth, at a speed of more than 11,000 kilometres per hour. The sheer force from the impact could destroy a large target with as much power as a nuclear bomb – but without the deadly radiation.

Another possibility in the future are antimatter weapons, which are currently being researched. Subatomic particles such as protons and electrons also have antiparticles (antimatter), which act in the opposite way to ordinary matter. An explosion occurs if particles and their antimatter collide, releasing enormous energy. Antimatter is so powerful that scientists believe just a tiny amount – less than one gram – could release more energy than an atomic bomb. However, the process of producing and storing antimatter is very difficult and expensive and this technology is unlikely to be turned into a usable weapon for decades, if at all.

Robotic warfare, on the other hand, is advancing quickly. Prototypes of several different robots already exist and they may be seen on battlefields as soon as 2020. These new robots will vary in form; they may resemble humans, animals or insects and mimic their physical movements. Depending on the model, they will be able to walk, run, bend, fly... and perhaps talk in 40 languages. Some will be large, but many will be small. An army of tiny robots could function like a swarm of bees or ants. 'Swarming' is a battle tactic that involves overcoming the enemy not by strength but by numbers.

In the future it is hoped that fewer lives will be lost during wars if robotics can advance enough to replace soldiers on the battlefield. But in the meantime, medical robots could find wounded soldiers and then transmit vital information about the soldier's condition back to a human controller. These robots could put a wounded soldier into a vehicle and treat him as he's being taken to hospital. "A robots revolution is upon us," says P W Singer. "We're not just talking about tens of thousands of today's robots, but tens of thousands of these prototypes and tomorrow's robots.... Flash forward 25 years, [and] those robots will be close to a billion times more powerful in their computing than today." Singer may be exaggerating here, but computing has steadily become faster and more efficient. It's even possible that some robots

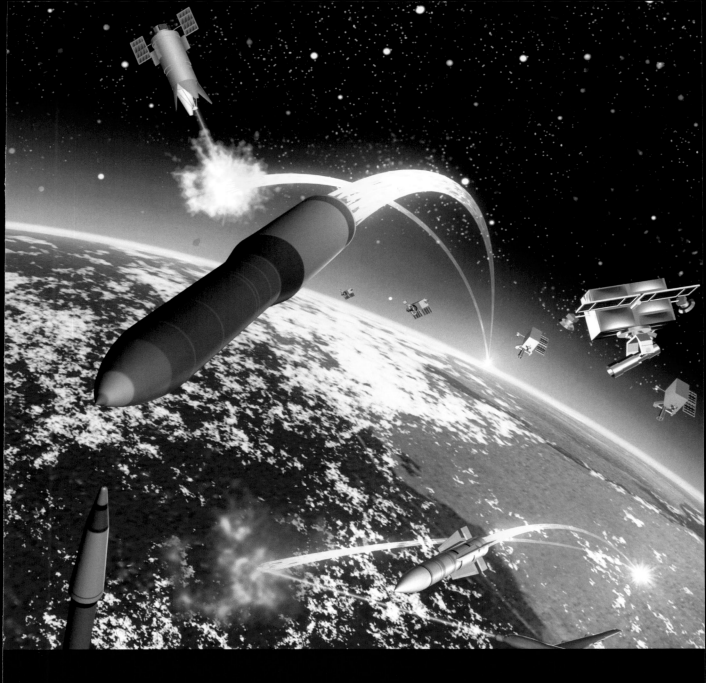

THE MILITARISATION OF SPACE

Satellites in space can take long-distance pictures that governments use to collect information about their enemies, such as showing whether they are amassing weapons. However, the Outer Space Treaty of 1967 prevents countries from placing WMD, such as nuclear weapons, in outer space. The Moon may not be used for military operations either. However, countries are allowed to place conventional weapons – such as missiles – in space. And military leaders say it is only a matter of time before war is waged in space, especially as more machines and robots are used in war. Space may turn out to be not only the final frontier but the next battlefront as well.

In the war against alien insect-bugs – really big ones that rule other planets – Ender Wiggin is Earth's great hope. In American author Orson Scott Card's 1985 novel Ender's Game, the governments of Earth select Ender to be a super warrior. He attends a special battle school where he is trained to fight in zero-gravity environments. He also uses a futuristic weapon of mass destruction called a 'molecular disruption device', which breaks the bonds of molecules in objects – even whole planets – and rips them apart. Ongoing advances in nanotechnology might make the so-called M.D. Device a possibility in real wars of the future.

will be preprogrammed to do things without the need for remote control. In 2010, US robotics scientist Robert Finkelstein stated, "Just as the catapult replaced human *muscle* in combat, intelligent robots can replace the human *mind*."

With the increasing use of robotics comes an increasing number of challenges – some practical and some ethical. For example, in the USA, the development of more unmanned vehicles and aeroplanes such as the Predator has created a problem: there are not enough qualified pilots. To solve the problem, the armed forces are starting to reach out to young people from the video game generation, as many adolescents who grew up playing computer or Xbox games already have many of the skills needed to operate a remote vehicle via a video feed. Some people worry that this distance – and the sense of detachment it creates – could be negative. Will soldiers find it easier to kill if they don't have to face their enemies in person? One US pilot acknowledges, "As anyone who's played *Grand Theft Auto* knows, we do things in the video world that we wouldn't do face to face." War is not a video game, but in the split-second that a video-fed soldier has to make a decision, he might not remember that.

Nanotechnology is a developing field that involves manipulating tiny particles – individual molecules or atoms. In warfare, nanotechnology could be used to build tiny weapons or to develop more powerful computers. Microscopic sensors could be used to

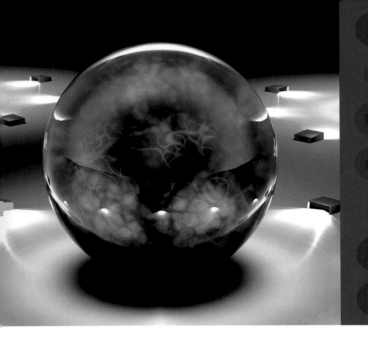

An artist's impression of nanotechnology – a manipulated particle (left). Although it remains a distant development, nanotechnology has the potential to create a new world – not only in warfare but also in communication and medicine.

detect potentially harmful chemicals, bacteria and viruses. In 2001, Kristofer Pister, a scientist at the University of California, Berkeley, came up with the idea of 'smart dust'. Tiny robotic sensors the size of grains of sand could be sprinkled over an area to send back information on enemy movements or to indicate the presence of radiation or poisonous gases. Nanotechnology could be used to change the molecular structure of a substance, altering its physical properties. For example, it could be used to make tank armour harder and more resistant to explosive devices. On the other hand, minuscule nanobots could be programmed to 'eat' certain materials, such as metal or rubber, to destroy weapons. It might even be possible to design nanobots that can be breathed in. These could be preprogrammed to 'read' a person's DNA and self-destruct if it matched a certain formula identifying the person as an enemy. Nanotechnology has potential medical applications, too. As of 2012, the US Air Force had a programme that was investigating how nanotechnology could be used to treat wounded personnel, using light and self-bonding materials to heal wounds in minutes.

TAKING AIM AT THE FUTURE

Is bigger better? For most of human history, war has been about size. Who has the bigger ships? The more powerful guns? The larger armies? In the 21st century and beyond, that may change. Military experts now believe that smaller may be the new ideal. Smaller aeroplanes and land vehicles are more mobile, require less power and are cheaper to produce. Rather than having a million soldiers, an army might do better with half or even a quarter of that number if those soldiers received specialised training and used improved equipment.

Perhaps the key word for military success in the future is 'agility'. Today, wars are fought not only on traditional battlefields but in houses, buildings and cities. It's likely that in the future, lines will be blurred even more. A big hurdle will be not technological but organisational – working out how to manage resources in new circumstances. And sometimes, it's not the fight that matters the most. It's restoring peace afterwards. As armed forces work with new governments and civilians to rebuild towns and societies, they will turn to communications technology to help them learn about foreign cultures and communicate in different languages.

Another challenge will be finding sufficient numbers of people who are extremely computer literate. As billions of pieces of sensitive information are exchanged in cyberspace, there will be billions of chances for it to fall into the wrong hands. Keeping information secure is critical in war, but cyberspace is one of the hardest places to achieve this. The locks and keys are all virtual.

Many of today's military personnel may never see an enemy face-to-face during war. Instead, they will be monitoring, analysing and securing information collected by computers.

CLICK HERE FOR WAR

Wars may be fought on the other side of the world, but people at home can still see what's happening. In 2007, the US military launched its own channel on the video-sharing website YouTube.com, where it posted videos of actual battles as well as footage of American soldiers helping citizens in Iraq. Unofficially, many personnel have posted their own videos of what they've seen or experienced. Some are even set to music. Although these videos are one way to try to influence public opinion and increase support for troops, many of them show unfiltered incidents of violence, which leads some to worry that people will become desensitised to war.

Nearly every cybersecurity system, belonging to corporations or military organisations, has been hacked into at one point or another. Often, the best people to find and fix this problem are the hackers. Unfortunately, as some of these hackers may have learned their skills through illegal activities, most armed forces are reluctant to hire criminals. In 2009, the US government started to focus resources on a new part of the armed forces called Cyber Command (CYBERCOM), in order to improve security in the country's military networks. Cyber Command recruits former hackers as well as the most able IT specialists and trains them to the highest standards. Cyber Command is set to grow in size and importance over the next few years.

The sheer amount of information travelling between combat zones and command centres could also be a drawback. Knowing an enemy's position and plans is helpful. However, future computers have the potential to bombard soldiers with information about every soldier in range, every suspicious-looking rock in the road, and every time the wind changes direction. Soldiers don't have the time to process all this information. Two centuries ago, Carl von Clausewitz, a Prussian general who wrote about military strategy, invented the term 'fog of war'. Men in battle did not always have the luxury of carefully weighing all options to make good decisions because they were not sitting at a desk with the freedom to think clearly. They were having to act 'in the heat of battle', surrounded by smoky air

and wounded comrades and without all the information they needed. Although computers and the Internet can provide billions of bits of information, they don't always sort through it, and this information overload can actually increase the fog of war.

For some technological advances, scientists don't yet have the knowledge to make them work. Research continues on how to improve robots' movement, vision and 'thinking'. Although robots can register vast amounts and more detailed information than humans, they are incapable of reasoning it all out. It's impossible to preprogram every situation a military robot might encounter. A huge area of research involves developing artificial intelligence that allows robots to 'think' for themselves. Part of this effort involves mapping

While some military robots may one day have enough artificial intelligence to operate independently, for now remote operators are still in full control of them.

WIKILEAKS: SECRE

SHELVED FOR SEAS

WEB WAR I

*The Internet was down. The computer system of the main bank wasn't working.
E-mails between government offices couldn't get through. In 2007, Estonia, a small
country in northern Europe, was the victim of a series of cyber attacks. Never before
had a country been attacked in so many places at once. It was also the first time
that an entire government had to step in to defend itself. The attacks came after a
disagreement between Estonia and Russia, although the Russian government denied
it was involved. Regardless of who was to blame, 'Web War I' showed how vulnerable*

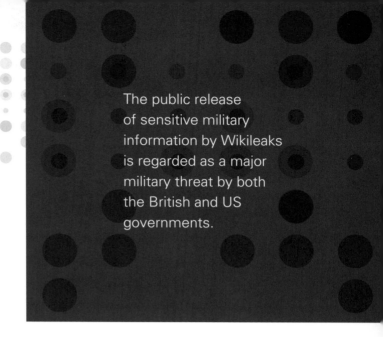

The public release of sensitive military information by Wikileaks is regarded as a major military threat by both the British and US governments.

the human brain to learn how it does what it does. Then, scientists could build software systems that imitate these processes. The idea of using armed robots in combat is controversial – especially when the technology does not exist to enable robots to act reliably. Joseph Dyer is a former US Navy officer who managed research and development of weapons systems. Today he works at iRobot, a robotics development company. "Having an armed robot deployed will require absolutely the best design, the most careful design, and the very best testing," Dyer says. "Will we see armed robots? Yes. But – [there is] a lot of work to be done."

Another hurdle will be powering robots built for war. Human muscles are tremendously capable when it comes to storing power and then using it when necessary. But no robotic machine comes close to being as efficient as a human body. In addition, some future robots are likely to be tiny. Miniature flying robots will need enough battery power to stay airborne, but the battery itself can't be so heavy as to pull them down. Advances in computer technology will help fit parts together more tightly and in smaller spaces. Improvements in nanotechnology could provide a huge boost as well. Researchers in China, Japan, Germany and the United States are working to build precision machines that can manipulate tiny particles and build mechanical parts and systems at an atomic level.

Besides technical challenges, there are other obstacles Money, of course, remains a problem that is as old as war itself. It's tremendously expensive to fund military research and then to produce the technology to put it into action. For example, antimatter weapons could be more powerful than any weapon known today. However, the cost to produce even a tiny amount of antimatter – less than what would be needed to power even a small weapon – runs into the billions. New weapons also raise legal and ethical concerns. Currently, using biological or chemical weapons is prohibited by treaty. This does not mean, of course, that no one will deploy them in the future. Governments will have to decide whether to play by the rules or, in some cases, rewrite them.

In *War Made New*, author Max Boot states, "... technology sets the parameters of the possible; it creates the *potential* for a military revolution." One way to advance technology is to make sure it has uses off the battlefield as well as on it. If military-oriented machines or software can also be used by cities, companies and private citizens, there will be a greater demand to develop them, and costs will be driven down. For example, one of iRobot's biggest clients isn't the military – it's homeowners who use the company's robotic vacuum cleaner! Yet historically, warfare fuelled much of our wider technological advancement, as we searched for ways to kill and destroy with greater efficiency. The hope is that future warfare will spare more lives, but changing the ways of war will not be a quick or easy process.

Although new technology can bring advantages to the battlefield, military leaders emphasise that it's important to train people in how to use them most effectively. As former US Army officer Robert Scales notes, "The greatest advantage can be achieved by out-thinking rather than out-equipping the enemy." The winners of future wars will be the combatants who not only have the best technology but who know how to use it.

They may not yet look like the robots of science-fiction films, but the era of robots has begun, both on battlefields (above) and in our homes (a cleaning robot, left).

GLOSSARY

anthrax a fatal bacterial disease that affects the skin and lungs

atomic bomb a bomb that generates an enormous explosion using atomic, or nuclear, energy, which is produced by the splitting or fusing of atoms, the tiny particles that make up an object

ballistic missile a long-range missile weapon that travels at sub-orbital heights (no more than 100 kilometres above the Earth)

battle zones the place where a battle takes place. This could be in the air, on land, at sea or in cyberspace

casualties injuries or fatalities suffered in war

civilian someone who is not officially involved in military action

collateral damage accidental death, injury or damamge caused by military weapons

DNA an organism's unique combination of genes, which are the hereditary units that determine the particular characteristics of the organism

improvised explosive devices (IEDs) homemade bombs made from a variety of materials; they are usually set off in an unexpected location, such as a roadside

infiltrate to invade in a secretive or stealthy manner

integrated to be thoroughly combined with something else, usually for a positive effect

lasers devices that control the movement of atoms to create electromagnetic radiation (usually in the form of light); the name stands for 'light amplification by stimulated emission of radiation'

malfunction to operate in a way not according to plan, usually with negative effects

navigate to establish a proper course of travel or action

parameters sets of conditions or limitations within which something happens

projectile weapon a weapon that fires a damaging object such as a bullet

prototypes the first working models of a new technology

radiation the process of sending out energy in the form of waves or particles; in excessive amounts, it can harm or kill living organisms

reconnaissance the act of gathering and sharing information

robot a machine that can work without a human controlling it.

satellites objects placed into Earth's orbit to receive and transmit information over long distances

sensors objects that can pick up and record data

surveillance the act of observing, often in secret, in order to gather information; commonly known as spying

telegraph an instrument invented in the 19th century that used electrical signals, coded with a series of dots and dashes, to send messages through wires

treaties agreements among countries or other global organisations

virtual relating to something done outside the physical realm but meant to achieve the effects of something done in reality

war zones see battle zones

FURTHER READING

EDGE: Ultimate 20: Weapons of War by Tracey Turner (Franklin Watts, 2013)

Both Sides of the Story: The Ethics of War by Patience Coster (Franklin Watts, 2013)

Ethical Debates: Military Intervention by Kaye Stearman (Wayland, 2012)

Our World Divided: Afghanistan From War to Peace by Philip Steele (Wayland, 2013)

War Made New: Technology, Warfare, and the Course of History, 1500 to Today by Max Boot (Gotham Books, 2012)

Drone Warfare: Killing by Remote Control by Benjamin Medea (revised edition, Verso, 2013)

Wired for War: The Robotics Revolution and Conflict in the Twenty-First Century by P W Singer (Penguin, 2009/2011)

WEBSITES

HowStuffWorks: How the Predator UAV Works

http://science.howstuffworks.com/predator.htm

This site provides a detailed but accessible explanation of the design and operation of the US Predator UAV, the drone that has been used extensively to find and attack terrorists.

iRobot

http://www.irobot.com/gi/

Visit this site to learn more about one of the world's leading robot manufacturers and to get a close look at the capabilities of military robots including the PackBot and Warrior.

INDEX

First published in the UK in 2013 by

Franklin Watts
338 Euston Road
London NW1 3BH

First published by Creative Education
P.O. Box 227, Mankato, Minnesota 56002
Creative Education is an imprint of The Creative Company
www.thecreativecompany.us
Copyright © 2013 Creative Education

ISBN: 978 1 4451 2379 0
Dewey number: 355'.02

A CIP catalogue record for this book is available from the British Library.

Printed in China

Franklin Watts is a division of Hachette Children's Books,
an Hachette Uk Company
www.hachette.co.uk

Design and production by The Design Lab
Art direction by Rita Marshall

Photographs by Alamy (Everett Collection Inc., incamerastock, GL Archive), Bigstock
(f8_studio, lawcain, Olivier), Dreamstime (Cuteillustrations, Jakub Jirsák, Giorgios
Kollidas, Marek Redesiuk), Getty Images (Mandel Ngan/AFP, Stan Honda/AFP, Rob
Magiera), U.S. Air Force (Brett Clashman, David Darkow, Angel DelCueto, Val Gempis,
Rick Goodfriend, Andrew Lee, Leslie Pratt, Anthony Sanchelli, Julianne Showalter,
Tiffany Trojca, Nick Wilson, Bobbi Zapka), U.S. Army (Aaron Allmon, ASI, Gina
Chiaverotti, DARPA, Brian Ferguson, Ryan Hallock, C. Todd Lopez, Mark Miranda,
Redstone Technical Test Center, Claire Heininger Schwerin/PEO C3T), U.S. Navy
(Josue L. Escobosa)

Cover: An F-15 Strike Eagle fighter jet over Afghanistan
Page 1: US soldiers in combat training with a mobile robot
Page 2: An AC-130 gunship releasing flares during a training exercise